BORING STUFF...

LAFF-O-TRONIC JOKE BOOKS! IS PUBLISHED
BY STONE ARCH BOOKS, A CAPSTONE IMPRINT
1710 ROE CREST DRIVE
NORTH MANKATO, MN 56003
WWW.CAPSTONEYOUNGREADERS.COM

ISBN: 978-1-4965-8216-4 (PAPERBACK)

DESIGNER: RUSSELL GRIESMER
EDITOR: DONALD LEMKE

Printed and bound in China.
1121 - 1122 - 1123

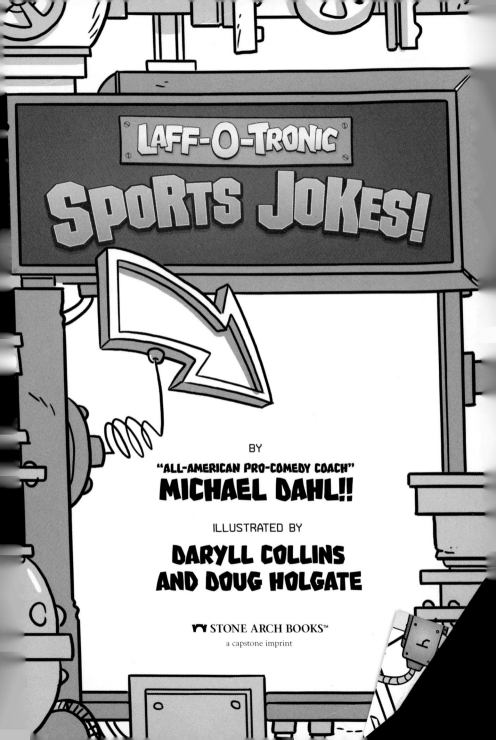

LAFF-O-TRONIC
SPORTS JOKES!

BY

"ALL-AMERICAN PRO-COMEDY COACH"
MICHAEL DAHL!!

ILLUSTRATED BY

DARYLL COLLINS
AND DOUG HOLGATE

STONE ARCH BOOKS™
a capstone imprint

PRESS TO START!

FYI: THIS IS A BOOK. BUTTONS DON'T WORK IN BOOKS. YOU WILL PROBABLY HAVE TO TURN THE PAGE.

Why was Cinderella thrown off the soccer team?

Because she ran away from the ball.

What do you call a pig that knows karate?

A pork chop!

What do you call a basketball player's pet chicken?

A personal fowl.

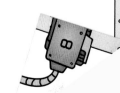

Why was Cinderella so bad at gymnastics?
Because she had a pumpkin for a coach.

What kind of cats like to go bowling?
Alley cats.

Did you hear about the race between the lettuce and the banana?

The lettuce was a head.

Who won the race between the two ocean waves?

They tide.

Where do golfers go after a game?

To a tee party.

Why shouldn't skaters tell jokes when they're racing?

Because the ice might crack up!

What did one soccer shoe say to the other?

Between us we're gonna have a ball!

What football team travels with the most luggage?

The Packers.

What football team spends the most money on their credit cards?

The Chargers.

A soccer player and a duck went out to dinner at a restaurant. But after dessert, the soccer player kicked the duck.

Why?

He said he would foot the bill.

Why is a baseball stadium always so cool?

Because it's full of fans.

What dessert should basketball players never eat?

Turnovers.

What mammal always shows up at a baseball game?

A bat.

Why didn't the golfer wear his new shoes on the golf course?

Because yesterday he got a hole in one.

What do you do when you see an elephant with a basketball?

Get out of his way!

What is the quietest sport in the world?
Bowling. You can hear a pin drop!

What game do sheep like playing?
Baaa-dminton.

What did the coach say to the broken candy machine?

Give me my quarterback!

What has 18 legs and catches flies?

A baseball team.

What is the hardest part about sky-diving?

The ground!

Why is tennis such a noisy game?

Because the players always raise a racket!

What do you call a guy who's good at wrestling?

MATT

What do you call a girl who's good at fishing?

ANNETTE

What do you call a guy who's great at scoring in volleyball?

SPIKE

What do you call a girl who's at the start of every boxing match?

BELLE

What do you call a guy who's good at catching fly balls?

MITT

What do you call a guy who's good at archery?

BO

MORE JOKES!

GRRR

WARNING!
DO NOT OPEN

HOCKEY PLAYER INSIDE

20

Why shouldn't a basketball player write a check?

Because it will probably bounce.

Why did the baseball hitter spend so much time at the playground?

He was working on his swing.

What famous baseball player lives under a tree?

Babe Root.

How is a hockey player like a magician?
They both do hat tricks!

Why are fish so bad at playing tennis?
They always run when they see a net!

Who's big, is a lumberjack, and runs marathons?
I give up.
Paul Bunion.

What do boxers and fishermen have in common?

They both land a hook in the jaw!

Never stand in front of an Olympic hurler.

Why, cuz I might get hit by the ball?

No, because he just had lunch!

What bird is good at boxing?

Duck.

Why did the bowling pins lie down?

They were on strike!

What position does Frankenstein play in hockey?

Ghoul keeper.

What is a cheerleader's favorite color?

Yeller!

Why is the receiver digging a pit in the middle of the football field?

The quarterback told him to "Go deep!"

Why did the tennis player carry a flashlight?

Because he always lost his matches!

What is the world's oldest sport?

Baseball. The Bible's first words are "In the big inning . . ."

Where do they serve food to football players?

In the Soup-er Bowl.

Where did the relay-racer wash his shoes?

In running water.

Why did the piano player join the baseball team?

Because he had perfect pitch.

Why was the nose so sad when his friends divided up into soccer teams?

Because it didn't get picked.

What did the football player say when he grabbed the duck?

"Touch down!"

How is a skydiver like a big game hunter?

They both like to chute.

What is harder to catch the faster you run?

Your breath!

When is a baby good at basketball?

When she's dribbling!

What do you call a pig who plays basketball?

A ball hog.

Why did the baseball owner hire elephants for his team?

Because they work for peanuts.

What do you call an astronaut who plays first base?

A SPACEMAN BASEMAN

What do you call a soccer player made of Swiss cheese?

A HOLEY GOALIE

What do you call
a wrestling match
between two pumped-
up fighters?

A MUSCLE TUSSLE

What do you call slime
on a basketball?

HOOP GOOP

What do you call a skateboarder who serves you dinner?

A SKATER WAITER

What do you call someone who pulls the football away at the very last moment?

A KICKER TRICKER

EXTREME PING-PONG

EXTREME THUMB WRESTLING

EXTREME DOMINOES

EXTREME JUMPING JACKS

EXTREME CROQUET

What do you call a boomerang that doesn't work?

A stick.

Why did the ballerina quit?

It was tu-tu hard!

What country holds the most marathons?

Iran.

Why are bullfights so noisy?

The bulls are always using their horns!

How do fireflies start a race?

"Ready. Set. Glow!"

Do you ever go rock climbing?

I would if I were boulder!

What is a runner's favorite subject in school?

Jography.

Why did the softball player bring her bat to the library?

Her teacher told her to hit the books!

Where can you find the largest diamond in the world?

On a baseball field.

What lights up a sports stadium?

A soccer match.

Which state has the most football uniforms?

New Jersey!

That robot must be a super athlete.

How can you tell?

Look at the size of that metal on his chest!

Where do elephants exercise?
At the jungle gym.

What do you call it when a T. rex makes a home run?
A dinoscore!

Why did the referee stop the zombie hockey game?

There was a face off in the corner.

Why couldn't the motorcycle racer pass the 18-wheeler?

Because it was two-tired!

What did the baseball glove say to the baseball?

"Catch you later."